123 SESAME STREET

MY FIRST 101 WORDS

Sky Pony Press books may be purchased in bulk at special discounts for sales promotion, corporate gifts, fund-raising, or educational purposes. Special editions can also be created to specifications. For details, contact the Special Sales Department, Sky Pony Press, 307 West 36th Street, 11th Floor, New York, NY 10018 or info@skyhorsepublishing.com.

Sky Pony® is a registered trademark of Skyhorse Publishing, Inc.®, a Delaware corporation.

Visit our website at www.skyponypress.com.

10 9 8 7 6 5 4 3 2 1

Library of Congress Cataloging-in-Publication Data is available on file.

Cover design by Daniel Brount
Interior photography by Getty Images

Print ISBN: 978-1-5107-6149-0
Ebook ISBN: 978-1-5107-6280-0

Printed in China

123

SESAME STREET®

MY FIRST 101 WORDS

Sky Pony Press
New York

Blue

Which of these colors am I?

Green

Red

Pink

Black

Yellow

White

Square

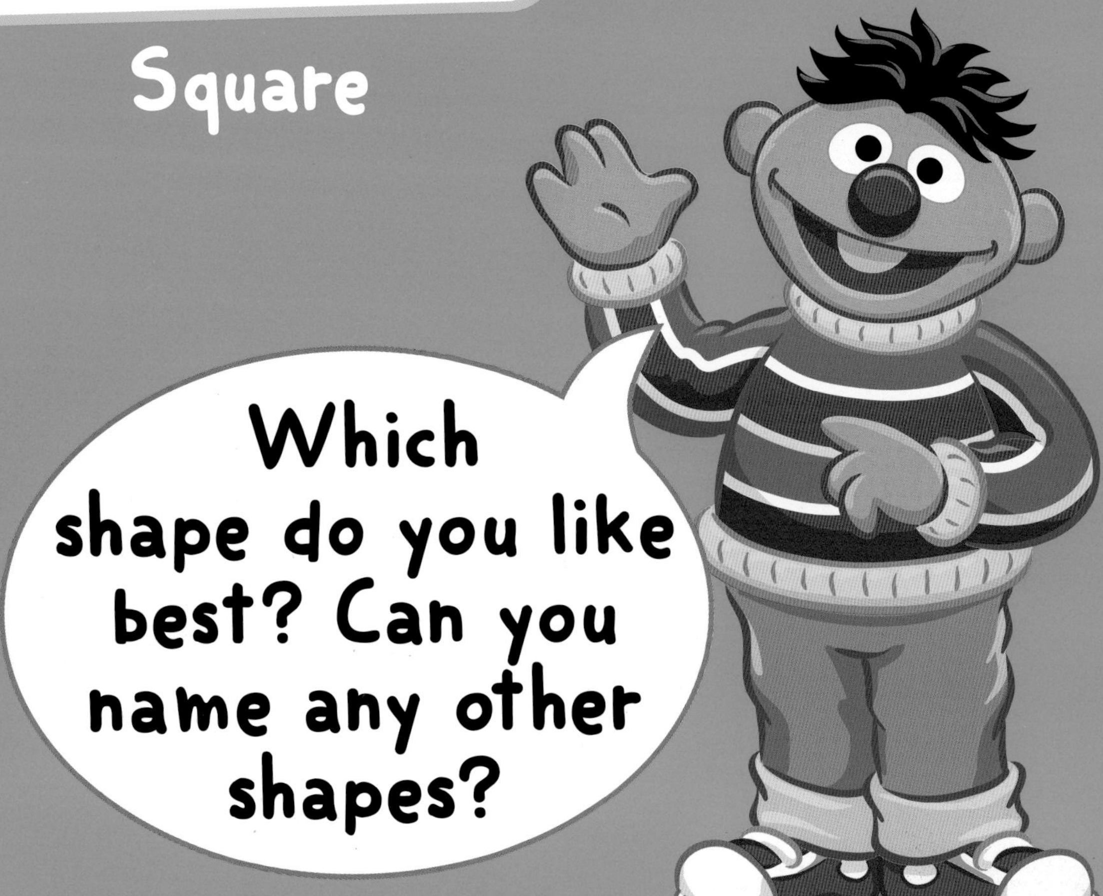

Circle

Triangle

One

Two

Three

Elephant

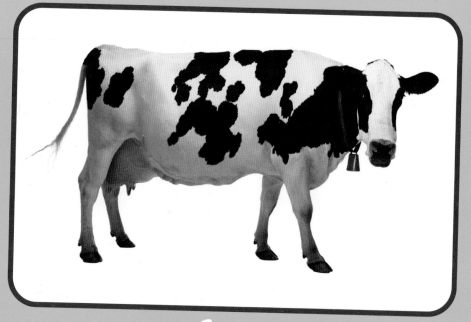

Cow

Monkey

Pig

Fox

Dog

Cat

Egg

Birds hatch from eggs!

Tree

Bird

Fish

Crab

Mouse

Ladybug

Moon

Where do we live?

Earth

Sun

Web

Nest

Cave

Girl

Boy

Mom

Dad

Legs

Arm

Hands

Lips

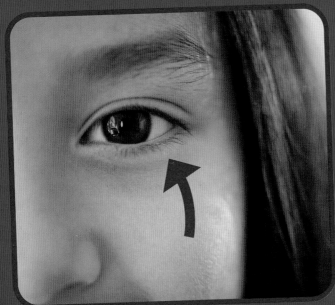

Eye

Nose

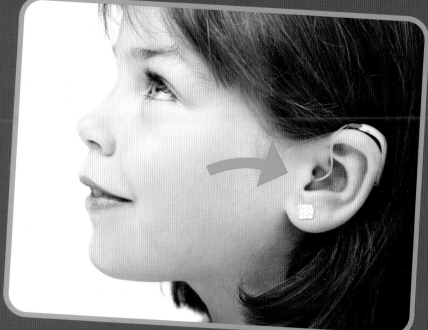

Ear

Hat

Gloves

Shoes

Which one goes on your head?

Dress

Pants

Shirt

Doctor

Police

Vet

Small

Big

Cold

Hot

In

Out

These are opposites—two things that don't belong together! Can you name any more?

Clean

Dirty

Book

Read

Sleep

Run

Walk

Skip

Jump

Movement is good for you! Everyone should move around and exercise every day.

Scared

Mad

Sad

Happy

Ham

Can

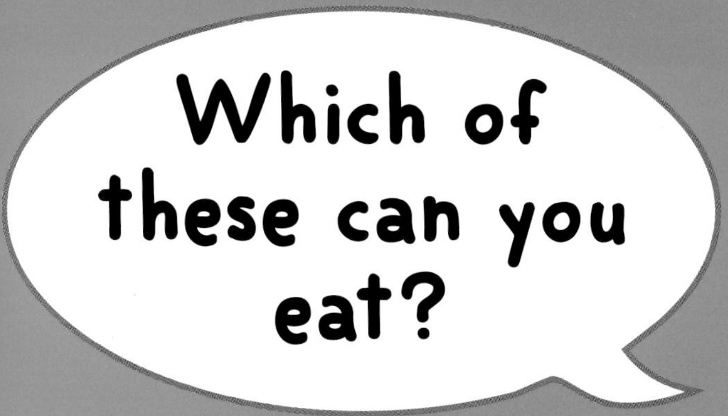

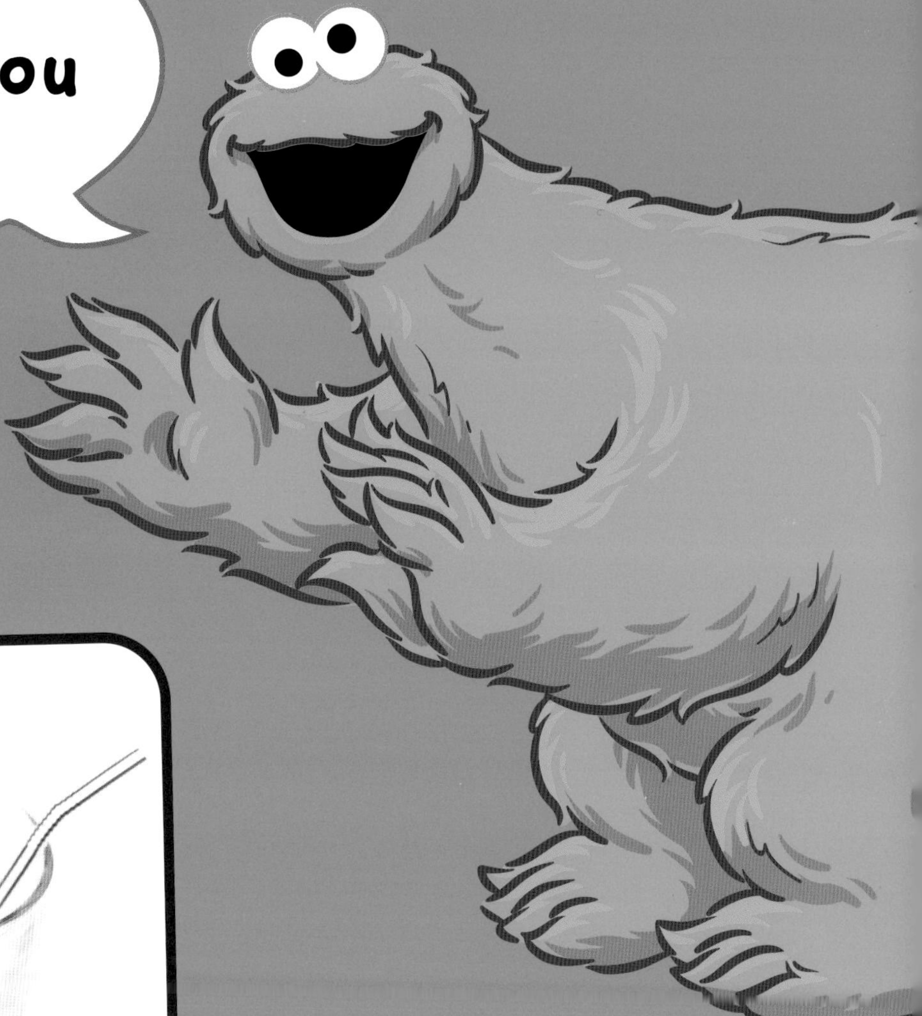

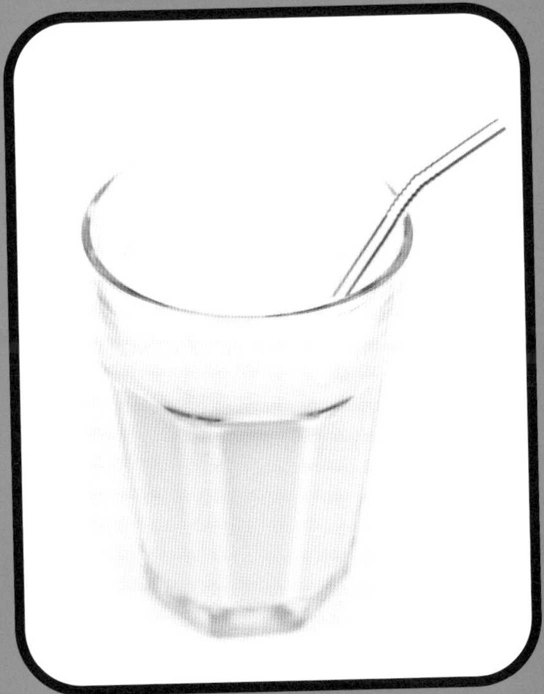

Cup

Milk

Cake

Bread

Banana

Apple

Cheese

Carrot

Spoon

Plate

Bowl

Pan

Which of these do you use to eat your food?

Pot

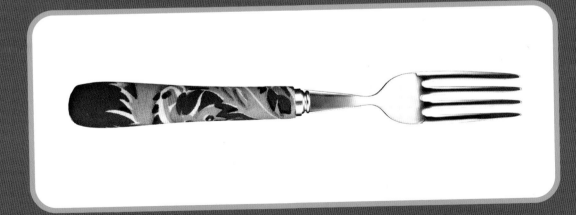

Fork

Bike

Car

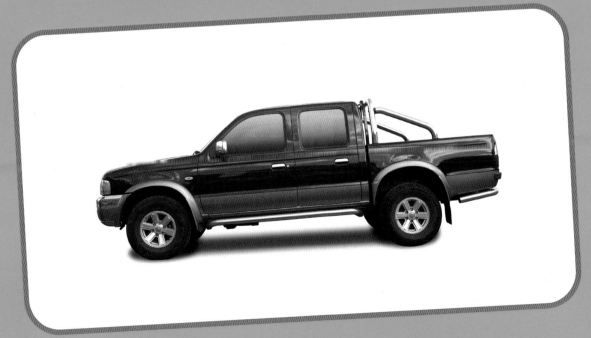

Truck

Plane

Which one of these do children ride to school?

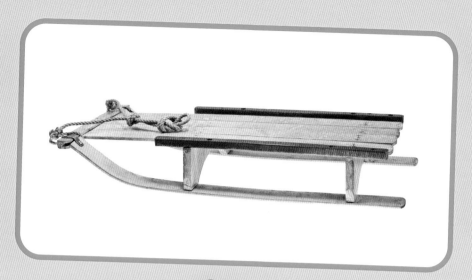

Sled

Bus

These are all things you can play with!

Ball

Bat

Doll

Block

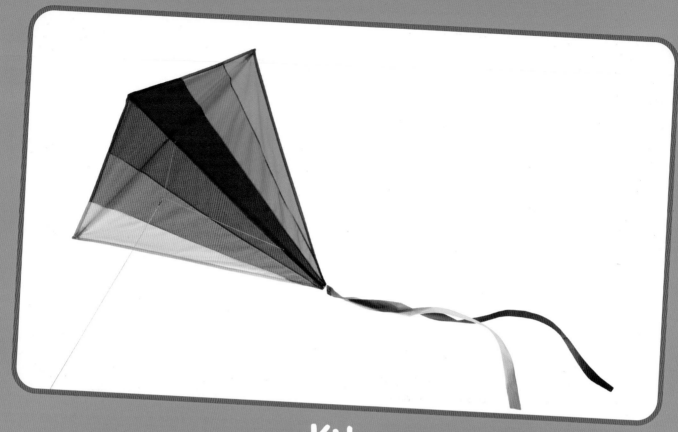

Kite

Which word starts with a B?

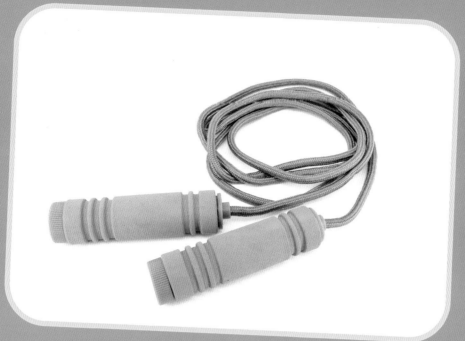

Jump Rope

Bear

Also Available

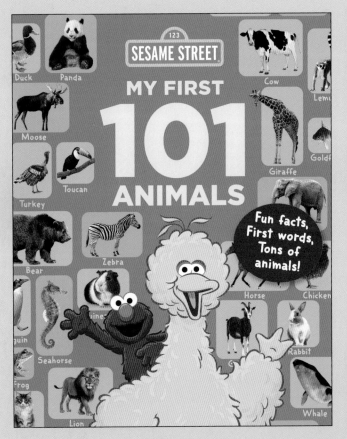